SPOTLIGHT ON
AN EQUITABLE WORLD

WORKING FOR FAIRNESS

Mary Ratzer

ROSEN
PUBLISHING

Published in 2025 by The Rosen Publishing Group, Inc.
2544 Clinton Street, Buffalo, NY 14224

First Edition

Editor: Greg Roza
Book Design: Michael Flynn

Photo Credits: Cover DC Studio/Shutterstock.com; cover, p. 3 (hands) Dedraw Studio/Shutterstock.com; (series Earth icon) v4ndhira/Shutterstock.com; p. 5 CarlosBarquero/Shutterstock.com; p. 6 insta_photos/Shutterstock.com; p. 7 Syda Productions/Shutterstock.com; p. 9 Dmytro Zinkevych/Shutterstock.com; p. 10 Veja/Shutterstock.com; p. 11 GeniusKp/Shutterstock.com; p. 13 Dragon Images/Shutterstock.com; p. 14 Rena Schild/Shutterstock.com; p. 15 https://commons.wikimedia.org/wiki/File:Lewis_and_clark-expedition.jpg/Shutterstock.com; p. 17 cadlikai/Shutterstock.com; p. 19 https://commons.wikimedia.org/wiki/File:13th_Amendment_Pg1of1_AC.jpg/Shutterstock.com; p. 20 https://commons.wikimedia.org/wiki/File:Warren_Court_(1953_-_1954).png; p. 21 Ground Picture/Shutterstock.com; p. 22 Linaimages/Shutterstock.com; p. 23 Mangostar/Shutterstock.com; p. 25 Everett Collection/Shutterstock.com; p. 26 Waheedullah Jahesh/Shutterstock.com; p. 27 solmaz daryani/Shutterstock.com; p. 29 lev radin/Shutterstock.com.

Cataloging-in-Publication Data

Names: Ratzer, Mary Boyd.
Title: Working for fairness / Mary Ratzer.
Description: Buffalo, NY : Rosen Young Adult, 2025. | Series: Spotlight on an equitable world | Includes glossary and index.
Identifiers: ISBN 9781499477306 (pbk.) | ISBN 9781499477214 (library bound) | ISBN 9781499477054 (ebook)
Subjects: LCSH: Fairness--Juvenile literature. | Interpersonal relations--Juvenile literature.
Classification: LCC BJ1533.F2 R38 2025 | DDC 179'.2--dc23

Manufactured in the United States of America

Some of the images in this book illustrate individuals who are models. The depictions do not imply actual situations or events.

CPSIA Compliance Information: Batch #CSRYA25. For further information contact Rosen Publishing at 1-800-237-9932.

CONTENTS

Chapter One

FAIRNESS IS EVERYBODY'S JOB

Look around at the real world. You can find evidence of fairness and unfairness. You can see that some people in the world have enough to meet their needs and thrive. You can see that some people don't have enough to meet their needs. Others have more than enough. Throughout history, many concerned individuals have put in the hard work to make progress toward fairness. But there is so much more work to be done.

You can see evidence of this through the work of abolitionists, civil rights activists, social reformers, United Nations response teams, advocates for a living wage, food pantry volunteers, and agencies supporting refugees and immigrants. They make a difference, turning hopelessness into hope.

Achieving fairness doesn't just happen overnight. Changing the way a society thinks is a big job, but it begins with you. You can be a positive force for good. Build connections between your feelings, values, and actions. Empathize with those who don't have what they need to thrive. Recognize that knowing more about people's lives and experiences helps you to become more aware of unfairness in the world. Look at bias and prejudice with an honest perspective. Open your eyes to the possibilities of making this a better world because you see problems and work to solve them. Use talents, tools, strengths, and allies to make fairness and equity happen. Set goals and work for positive change.

You don't have to work for fairness by yourself. The world is full of caring, empathetic people just like you!

Chapter Two

ACTIVE CITIZENS

A key goal for educators today is teaching and fostering the skills needed for active citizenship. In 2023, the National Assessment of Educational Progress showed that only 13 percent of eighth-graders are proficient in history. The standardized test also showed the first-ever drop in civics knowledge among the same students. Educational leaders recognize that civic education is essential for creating active citizens. Active citizens can make the difference between fairness and inequity by participating in their communities and being ready to solve problems.

You can learn to value fairness and empathy, growing compassion and respect for the needs of others. Thinking about the needs of others may motivate you to act. By envisioning yourself as an active participant in your community, you may be more willing to contribute to solving problems. These are building blocks for fairness.

Put in the work to learn more about inequity in your community. Awareness can lead to real change.

Young people growing into active citizenship develop skills, mindsets, and knowledge. Tools for active citizenship include familiar skills, such as using media, communication, and critical thinking. Working for what is important and meaningful can be rewarding! Having a willingness to learn from new perspectives and experiences helps you develop awareness inside and outside the classroom.

Pay attention to signs of equity and inequity in your real world. This helps builds awareness and understanding that could eventually lead to change. You might even be part of making change happen. Many young people have succeeded in creating equitable and fair solutions for problems. Using their voices, they worked for fairness and motivated others to do the same.

Chapter Three

FAIRNESS AT WORK

Everyone everywhere deserves to thrive. To build a just and caring world, many people work to close the distance between those who have what they need to survive and those who don't. Young people certainly contribute to this effort in their schools and communities. By paying attention to those in need, you can inspire a caring response in others. You can take action through planning, collaboration, and becoming an ally.

Many students are walking in the footsteps of inspiring and dedicated people. They are working to support those who need shelter, food, clothing, shoes, or a place to belong. Schools across the United States launch enthusiastic efforts for food drives and distribution. Volunteers from the community such as Girl Scout troops or church youth groups donate their energy and skills. Many students give their time and talents as mentors, coaches, tutors, and supportive neighbors. Younger community contributors often go on to maintain an active role as adults. They also share insight and awareness from their unique perspective. Step by step, this generosity leads to increased equity.

Connecting with community agencies with a focus on action can give you a direct link to service opportunities. Take, for instance, the Youth Community Action Network (Youth CAN) located in Buffalo, New York. This is a teen leadership group focused on promoting civic engagement. Teens plan and conduct community improvement projects. Organizations such as the Boy Scouts, Girl Scouts, Habitat for Humanity, YMCA, and Special Olympics engage young volunteers in community service. Service clubs in schools harness the energy and skills of volunteers to benefit the community.

Teens involved with Youth CAN meet twice a week to discuss community issues and plan community projects. In the past, they have reached out to homeless people with resources and developed a program to deter hate crimes.

Chapter Four

PAYING ATTENTION TO THOSE IN NEED

It's important to have something called social awareness when striving to achieve fairness in a society. This means paying attention and learning from experiences, differences, and observations. It's also important to open a connection to those around you who don't have what they need. Many people choose to ignore those in need. Engaging with the reality in front of you is a learning experience and a challenge. Ask yourself, "Can I do something to solve this problem?"

Have you ever noticed anyone without enough money trying to pay for the food they need? Maybe they have to put items back at the grocery store and leave, facing another day without enough to eat. As COVID-19-related supplemental food programs end, families must seek out food pantries in the community. Those who have the means

Prom is an important event for many teens, but preparing for prom can be expensive. Charitable organizations, such as Becca's Closet in Pompano Beach, Florida, collect and distribute dresses to high school girls who can't afford to buy a nice prom dress on their own.

have filled those shelves with food for people who don't have enough. During the height of the COVID-19 pandemic, U.S. Congress made school lunches free for all students regardless of their family's income level. When the funds for this program ran out, many school districts returned to offering free meals to only low-income students. The families in these districts faced a crisis that became a cause for action in many states. Legislatures passed laws that created new opportunities for hungry families.

You can also help members in your community by donating and sharing sports equipment, winter coats, shoes, clothes, books, safe spaces, mentors, tutors, prom gowns, or health care. Some community schools provide free stores so families can close the gap between enough and not enough. After-school programs in many cities close the gap with positive and supportive volunteers, social connections, academic help, fun, and dinner.

Chapter Five

CREATIVITY AND DESERTS

Deserts are so dry that very little can grow or live in them. They make survival difficult. Many people live in something called a food desert. This is a location that has fewer food resources than other places, even in the same town or city. Food deserts have fewer grocery stores and food delivery services, but also limited nutritious, affordable foods.

Some people live in food deserts, making survival difficult. Others live in book deserts, transportation deserts, healthcare deserts, and dental care deserts. There are places without housing options, social services, law enforcement, and vital supports for a safe, healthy life. These barriers prevent people from accessing what they need for wellbeing. Poverty is often a factor.

There are many creative and inspiring solutions to deserts such as these. The best place to start to solve the issue is by raising awareness of the problem. In many places, communities have joined together to bring in fresh, healthy food where there are no grocery stores. Students have assisted with school food gardens, weekend farmers markets, and food drives. Community gardens, even urban and rooftop gardens, and new stores have taken down the barriers to healthy food.

Rania Zuri, a young student in West Virginia, heard about book deserts when she was very young and decided to start a charity to put books into children's hands with amazing success. This same kind of effort can bring health care to rural areas, urban communities, and even community schools with volunteer doctors, nurses, dentists, dental hygienists, and other community helpers.

The COVID-19 pandemic hurt many local economies. Some grocery stores were forced to close branches—permanently or temporarily—resulting in food deserts.

Chapter Six

UNFAIR IDEAS, UNFAIR ACTIONS

There are barriers to fairness in many societies. Sometimes rules, laws, and ideas ignore the needs and rights of groups and individuals. Colonizers, governments, kings, and presidents have long decided that wealth, property, and power justified making sweeping societal changes that resulted in unfairness for many people.

Let's look back at the ideas that caused centuries of unfairness to the Native Americans. The leaders and citizens of our growing nation believed they had the right to claim what was valuable. They believed in their destiny to take what they valued from other groups. They believed the rights of others could be swept away.

To this day, Native Americans are still fighting for their rights and sovereignty. They've made great strides in the struggle for fairness, but they still face many obstacles.

This painting, *Lewis and Clark on the Lower Columbia* (1905), depicts a meeting between the Lewis and Clark expedition and Native Americans.

In 1803, President Thomas Jefferson sent explorers Merriweather Lewis and William Clark to the Western United States to claim territory for the country. Many of the Indigenous people already living in the region didn't believe people should own the land because it was to be shared respectfully. The claims European colonizers placed on American lands contributed to centuries of unfairness, broken treaties, and lost homelands for the Indigenous Americans. Unwilling to share the land with the Native people of the Americas, the governments and militaries took it.

The U.S. government moved Indigenous people by force to areas that were often very different from their homelands. The colonizers waged war on the Indigenous people. This injustice resulted in millions of Native Americans without homes, identity, and rights. Fighting back, thousands of Native people died.

Chapter Seven

COLONIZERS

European colonizers came to the New World and took whatever had value. Land, resources, and lives are still being taken by those who ignore rights and justice. Experts think that when Spanish explorer Christopher Columbus sailed to the Americas in 1492, there were about 60 million Indigenous people living in North and South America. Drastic reduction of populations happened as the Spanish conquistadors claimed parts of Central and South America. The number of Inca, Aztec, and Maya people greatly decreased after wave after wave of Europeans seeking gold and riches. Disease, loss of land and resources, enslavement, and terror destroyed the lives of millions of Native Americans.

Consider the words of the respected Oglala Lakota chief, Red Cloud: "They made us many promises, more than I can remember, but they never kept but one; they promised to take our land, and they took it." Wars waged on Native peoples took away the identity, culture, land, and lives by the millions. By 1900 in the United States, the Native American population reached a desperate low of about 237,000. When colonizers and those who took up their quest arrived on the continent, experts think that North America had between 1 and 18 million people across the United States and Canada. Today, there are nearly 11.5 million Native people in the two countries.

What do these numbers mean? Colonizers came, claimed, took, displaced, destroyed, and often thrived. Holding beliefs that they were destined to conquer cultures they deemed below them, colonizers justified their actions. This concept was known as Manifest Destiny.

The land that now makes up Grand Teton National Park was once the home of the Eastern Shoshone peoples. The U.S. government relocated them east to the Wind River Indian Reservation in 1868.

Chapter Eight

LESS EQUAL, MORE EQUAL

The treatment of enslaved people and immigrants are another part of the United States's history of unfairness, which continues today.

For hundreds of years in the United States, slave labor made it possible for wealthy landowners to raise crops and grow rich in many states. For hundreds of years, without empathy or justice for millions, the white landowners violated the basic human rights of enslaved people. They denied them freedom, literacy, family bonds, and dignity. Enslaved people were legally considered property and not humans. They were owned and used for profit. The work of abolitionists and some government leaders tried to end this injustice on December 6, 1865, when the 13th Amendment to the Constitution was made law.

However, even after the 13th Amendment was enacted, other laws, policies, and practices took away the rights of people based on race. Barriers blocked and still block basic rights, equitable education, home ownership, economic opportunities and jobs, voting rights, and even access to health care.

Immigrants seeking safety, work, and basic needs often face a desperate struggle for acceptance and fair treatment. The United States decided in 1882 to stop allowing Chinese immigrants to come to the country. This was the first of many bans or limits on immigrants who often did the hardest and most dangerous jobs, lived in the poorest shelters, and faced hunger, prejudice, and inhuman treatment. Even the term "illegal alien" today reflects a lack of human dignity and fair treatment to people struggling to survive in the Unites States.

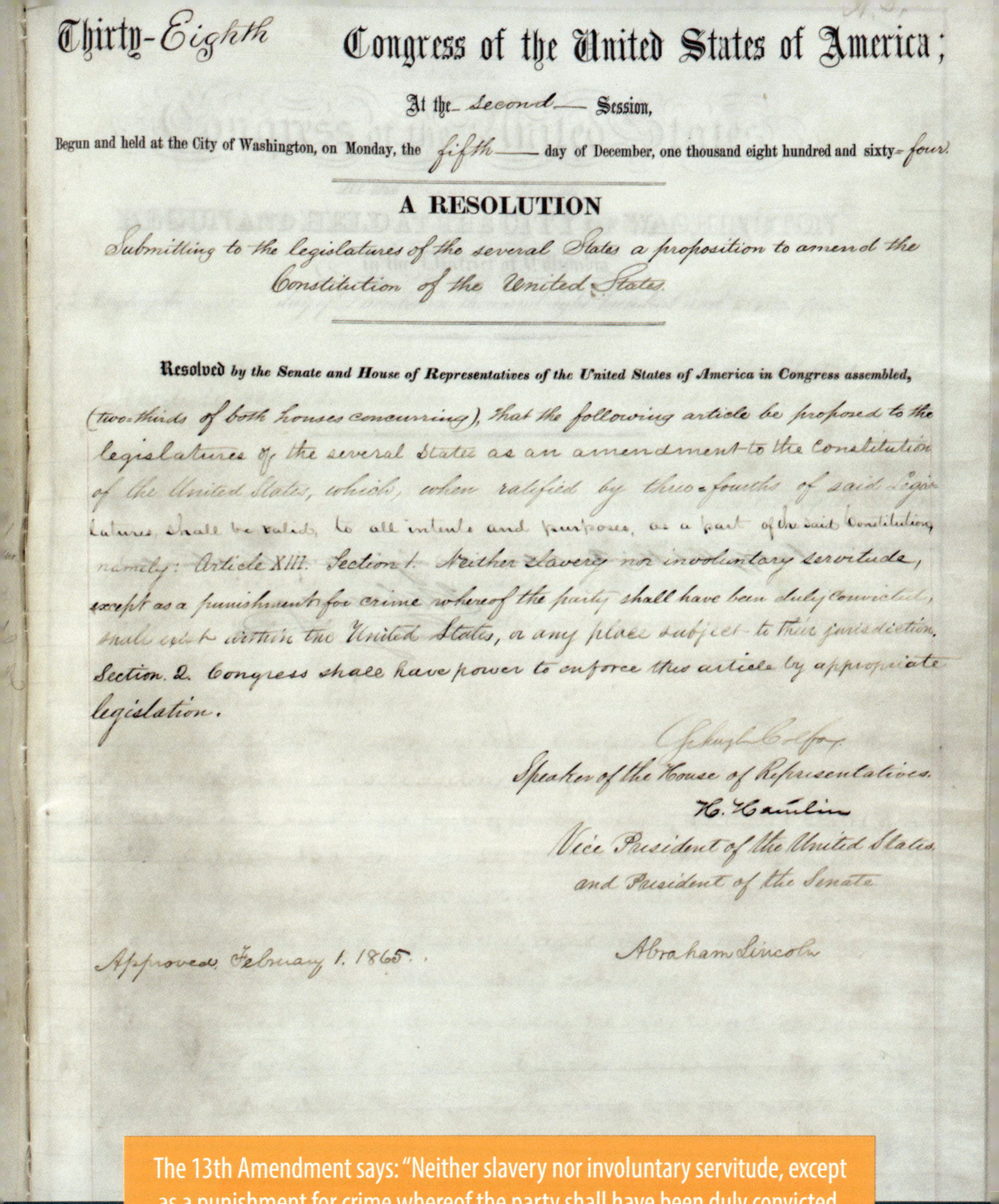

Thirty-Eighth Congress of the United States of America;

At the Second Session,

Begun and held at the City of Washington, on Monday, the fifth day of December, one thousand eight hundred and sixty-four.

A RESOLUTION

Submitting to the legislatures of the several States a proposition to amend the Constitution of the United States.

Resolved by the Senate and House of Representatives of the United States of America in Congress assembled, (two-thirds of both houses concurring), that the following article be proposed to the legislatures of the several States as an amendment to the Constitution of the United States, which, when ratified by three-fourths of said Legislatures, shall be valid, to all intents and purposes, as a part of the said Constitution, namely: Article XIII. Section 1. Neither slavery nor involuntary servitude, except as a punishment for crime whereof the party shall have been duly convicted, shall exist within the United States, or any place subject to their jurisdiction. Section 2. Congress shall have power to enforce this article by appropriate legislation.

Schuyler Colfax
Speaker of the House of Representatives.

H. Hamlin
Vice President of the United States, and President of the Senate

Approved, February 1. 1865.

Abraham Lincoln

The 13th Amendment says: "Neither slavery nor involuntary servitude, except as a punishment for crime whereof the party shall have been duly convicted, shall exist within the United States, or any place subject to their jurisdiction."

Chapter Nine

EQUAL PROTECTION UNDER THE LAW

The U.S. Constitution guarantees equal protection under the law for all Americans, but the country hasn't always extended the same rights to all people. Even after the 13th Amendment, many people were segregated and denied opportunities because of their race. People of color couldn't live, work, and go to school in the same places as white Americans.

In 1954, the Supreme Court ruled that separate is not equal in its *Brown v. Board of Education of Topeka* decision. Our democracy upholds these principles that defeated segregation, or the existence of separate schools for white children and Black children. Despite the ruling, there are still those in the United States who say: "What about us?"

All justices serving in the Supreme Court in 1954, shown here, ruled that racial segregation was unconstitutional.

Students at low-income schools often don't have access to advanced technology, such as robotics, leaving them a step behind their peers in education.

Many young people, especially those living in poverty, still don't receive an education equal to their fellow Americans. Oftentimes, these low-income schools serve a higher percentage of people of color compared to wealthier school districts. Health issues, language, and adverse experiences are part of the picture. Student absenteeism and a lack of motivation are barriers to success. Violence can occur in the neighborhoods near urban schools, adding to stress. Schools address all that they can, but demand exceeds resources. Students need a safe learning environment to engage with school responsibilities.

Suburban schools where middle class families live often provide options for their students that result in high graduation rates, support for learners who need it, and a safe learning environment. Often the teachers' resources in these schools support challenging course work, higher-level thinking, engaging subject matter, dependable technology, and preparation for college or work. Funding comes from school taxes on valuable properties and comfortable homes. This often results in safe environments that foster learning and creativity.

Chapter Ten

GOT THE SKILLS, GOT THE JOB

One way a lack of fairness shows up in society is in the workplace. Many employers require a college degree, which can deny qualified people employment opportunities. This even happens when job seekers had been succeeding at the same job in another place. The rising cost of college has put a degree out of reach for many.

Because of the demand for workers is high in many places now, a shift has happened. State governments in Maryland, Pennsylvania, Georgia, Utah, and New York are hiring workers based on skills, not necessarily their educational background. Companies such as Google, Walmart, Boeing, General Motors, and Apple are doing the same. Not having a degree may no longer be a barrier for people whose skills match the job.

A college degree is certainly an asset for someone looking for a job, but it shouldn't be the only criteria employers expect from workers. Real-world experience is also an asset.

On his first day in office, Pennsylvania governor Josh Shapiro signed an order to make thousands of government jobs open to people without a four-year college degree. Maryland no longer requires degrees for almost 50 percent of its positions, opening thousands of jobs in healthcare, corrections, policing, skilled trades, and engineering.

More than half of all Americans 25 years old and older don't have any type of college degree, yet many have quality skills in their respective fields. Many learned their skills in the military, in on-the-job training, or in trade schools. Hiring based on skills benefits rural workers and those experiencing poverty who often can't afford college. It also benefits Black and Hispanic job seekers who are less likely to have a degree compared to white or Asian applicants. The financial cost of attaining a college degree has blocked many people from good salaries and success. Equity breaks the barriers to fairness that keep many from possibilities they deserve.

Chapter Eleven

HISTORIC ACTION FOR FAIRNESS

Evidence of meaningful and hard-won progress for equity can be seen throughout the United States over the past century.

- **Education:** In 1920, only one in six young Americans finished high school. Many still worked on farms instead of going to school. Less than 1 percent of adults 23 years old and older had a college degree. In the 2019–2020 school year, the high school graduation rate was 87 percent and more than 37 percent of people aged 25 and older had at least a bachelor's degree.
- **Women:** In 1920, most women stayed home and raised children. Some worked in factories or mills. They had just gained the right to vote. Some women who fought for the right to vote were imprisoned and mistreated. During World War II, the nation needed laborers, and women became valued workers for the war effort. After the war, many women stayed in the work force and earned a living independently. Women still advocate for equal pay for equal work since they earn less than men in the same job in some industries.
- **Workers:** Prior to 1920, workers often had a six-day work week, working up to 60 hours. The average pay at this time was about $27 a week. Labor unions bargained for safer working conditions, shorter work weeks, and more salary. Advocates took action for equity through picketing and even strikes. Some children still worked in coal mines and other dangerous jobs. Advocates raised awareness and succeeded in positive change. Today, flexible work hours, job sharing, protections for safe workplaces, laws working toward a living wage, and fairness in treatment of workers are all the result of action for fairness.

Many women proved themselves as capable workers during World War II, when many men were fighting in the war. This helped increase the presence of women in all kinds of industries.

Chapter Twelve

HEROIC STRUGGLE FOR EQUITY

When the U.S. military pulled out of Afghanistan in the summer of 2021, girls' schools became a target for Taliban leaders. In 2021, there were 1.1 million Afghan girls in secondary school.

In Kabul, 256 girls from a school there made a desperate escape. Stuck in Kabul airport, their teachers and administrators burned student records to protect them from harm. The school was taken over and the students faced terror. The founder of the school, Shabana Basij-Rasikh, received support from around the world to recreate her school. Determined to provide an education for these girls, the School of Leadership Afghanistan (SOLA), successfully moved to Rwanda. A

A girl attending school in Kabul, Afghanistan, in 2022.

This photograph from 2019 shows a girls' school in Herat, Afghanistan. In 2024, schools like these no longer exist in the country.

school where the students could learn in safety opened the doors to a future of possibilities. Without an education beyond Grade 6, girls in Afghanistan could never reach their potential. Poverty, early marriage, and hopelessness define the lives of the girls who were left behind.

In Rwanda, Afghan girls become the best educated in the history of their native country. With a dedication to providing a sense of purpose and respect for themselves and others, this school prepares confident and caring leaders. They see beyond beliefs that created barriers. They recognize their responsibility to each other and the girls who do not have the opportunity to learn and achieve.

Chapter Thirteen

FOOD FOR THOUGHT

Take a minute to consider the perspectives of people dedicated to fairness. Their actions provide a wakeup call for a better world.

- **Andrew Carnegie** came to the United States from Scotland as an immigrant in 1848. At 13, he earned $1.20 a week working in a cotton mill. He achieved amazing success in industry, becoming the richest man in the United States. He sold his company for $480 million dollars in 1901 and throughout the rest of his life gave away $350 million. His belief was that beyond paying for your needs, wealth should be used to benefit the community. He advised all with these words: "To try to make the world in some way better than you found it is to have a noble motive in life."
- **Robert Hale** is a billionaire who was the commencement speaker for graduation ceremonies at the University of Massachusetts in 2023. Hale gave each of the 2,500 graduates two envelopes, each with $500 dollars in them. He urged the young adults to keep one and give the other to someone else in need. Hale gave away $2.5 million to encourage charitable efforts and spread the message of empathy for others.
- **St. Jude's Children's Research Hospital** treats children with life-threatening illness at no cost to families. In 2022, 730 refugee children from Ukraine with cancer were treated for free at St. Jude's and at hospitals in Europe. Generous contributions made this possible.

In another inspiring case from 2019, billionaire, inventor, and philanthropist Robert Smith pledged to pay off the student loans of the graduating class of Morehouse College that year—an estimated $34 million!

Chapter Fourteen

THINK GLOBALLY, ACT LOCALLY

Every human being has the right to the resources they need to thrive. How would children your age answer these questions in your city, state, the United States, Central America, Sudan, Ukraine, India, Iraq, Central African Republic, Afghanistan, Syria, or Somalia?

- **Do I know what is fair? Do I know I have rights?**
- **Am I free? Am I enslaved? Do I have to work to eat?**
- **Can I go to school? Can I go to college?**
- **Am I hungry? Are people starving here?**
- **Do I have enough water? Is my water safe?**
- **Is the air I breathe healthy and safe?**
- **Am I safe? Am I in danger because of violence?**
- **Can I make choices about my future?**
- **Can I get health care?**
- **Will I have the right to vote?**

Apathy and indifference make it hard to achieve fairness. Paying attention to the actions of others working to achieve fairness can be be a source of inspiration. So many people working to solve a problem look around and find allies in their efforts.

Challenge yourself to understand unfairness. Compare and contrast the work being done for equity and the work still needed. Map your awareness of the world around you as you learn, and build your understanding of it and the people in it. Make the choice to seek justice for the people in your community and the world.

GLOSSARY

abolitionist: A person who wants to abolish, or stop, slavery.

advocate: To support a cause or proposal; also, a person who supports a cause.

apathy: A lack of emotion or concern.

bias: To have an unfair preference or dislike of something.

civics: A social science dealing with the rights and duties of citizens.

equity: Fairness or justice in dealings between persons or groups.

immigrant: A person who leaves one country and comes to another country to live there.

inequity: Injustice in dealings between persons or groups.

philanthropist: Someone who makes an active effort to promote human welfare, often with donations of money.

picket: For workers to protest an employer outside a place of work, and trying to persuade others not to enter during a strike.

prejudice: Unfriendly feelings directed against an individual, a group, or a race.

refugee: An individual who has left his or her native country and is unwilling or unable to return to it because of persecution or fear of persecution.

Taliban: A fundamentalist Islamic military group in Afghanistan.

volunteer: Offer to do something for free.

INDEX

ROSEN Verified

THE BILL OF RIGHTS

What Are States' Rights?

Published in 2024 by The Rosen Publishing Group, Inc.
2544 Clinton Street, Buffalo, NY 14224

First Edition

Editor: Greg Roza
Book Design: Michael Flynn

Photo Credits: Cover Moab Republic/Shutterstock.com; (series background) PinkPueblo/Shutterstock.com; pp. 5, 35, 37 courtesy of the Library of Congress; p. 7 https://commons.wikimedia.org/wiki/File:Shays_forces_flee_Continental_troops,_Springfield.jpg; p. 9 https://en.wikipedia.org/wiki/File:John_Jay_(Gilbert_Stuart_portrait).jpg; p. 11 https://commons.wikimedia.org/wiki/James_Madison#/media/File:James_Madison.jpg; p. 13 https://commons.wikimedia.org/wiki/File:Hamilton_Trumbull_1792-retouch.jpg; p. 15 Sean Pavone/Shutterstock.com; p. 17 https://commons.wikimedia.org/wiki/File:Thomas_Hobbes_by_John_Michael_Wright_(2).jpg; p. 19 Sergey Novikov/Shutterstock.com; p. 21 EQRoy/Shutterstock.com; p. 23 Mr. Louis/Shutterstock.com; p. 25 Jude Schroder/Shutterstock.com; p. 27 Ringo Chiu/Shutterstock.com; p. 29 https://commons.wikimedia.org/wiki/File:Elbridge_Gerry_by_James_Barton_Longacre,_c._1820,_drawing,_from_the_National_Portrait_Gallery_-_NPG-NPG_77_297Gerry-000001.jpg; p. 31 eurobanks/Shutterstock.com; p. 33 https://commons.wikimedia.org/wiki/File:%22Surrender_of_General_Lee.%22.jpg; p. 39 Wangkun Jia/Shutterstock.com; p. 41 Satakorn/Shutterstock.com; p. 43 Sascha Burkard/Shutterstock.com; p. 45 MikeDotta/Shutterstock.com.

Cataloging-in-Publication Data

Names: Keppeler, Jill.
Title: What are states' rights? / Jill Keppeler.
Description: New York : Rosen Publishing, 2024. | Series: Rosen verified: the Bill of Rights | Includes glossary and index.
Identifiers: ISBN 9781499469813 (pbk.) | ISBN 9781499469820 (library bound) | ISBN 9781499469837 (ebook)
Subjects: LCSH: States' rights (American politics)--Juvenile literature. | Federal government--United States--Juvenile literature.
Classification: LCC JK311.K47 2024 | DDC 320.473'049--dc23

Manufactured in the United States of America

CONTENTS

Fabric of the Country

The U.S. Bill of Rights is the first 10 amendments, or changes, to the U.S. **Constitution**. When many people think of this list, they think of rights like the freedom of speech. Maybe they think of the right to bear arms. Those are very important rights to the people of the United States.

The Ninth and Tenth Amendments of the Bill of Rights aren't as **specific**. They usually don't appear in court decisions. But they're key to the whole story of the Bill of Rights. They're important to the fight for the new constitution. While these amendments aren't as well-known, they're rooted deep in the history of the country.

Back in 1787, **delegates** arrived for the Constitutional **Convention** in Philadelphia, Pennsylvania. They knew things were going to change in the young United States. The next four years were full of those changes. People had very different opinions on the Constitution and what it needed. The Bill of Rights was meant to help mend these differences. Some people think the Ninth and Tenth Amendments don't have much to do with law these days. However, they're still very much part of the fabric of the country.

The Bill of Rights, the U.S. Constitution, and the Declaration of Independence are kept at the National Archives in Washington, D.C.

Constitutional Convention

The delegates who met in 1787 in Philadelphia meant to change the old constitution. This document, or piece of writing, was called the Articles of Confederation. It didn't give the federal, or central, government much power. Leaders couldn't govern the new country well. Delegates decided to write a new constitution.

People had many disagreements about this. Some still didn't want the federal government to have power. They remembered the ways the king in Great Britain treated the colonies. Still, the government needed enough power to be able to do its job. The new constitution gave it this power.

Shays's **rebellion** in 1786 and 1787 was the last straw for the Articles of Confederation. The federal government couldn't raise the money or people to put down the rebellion itself. Leaders knew something had to change.

WASHINGTON & CO.

All the states in 1787 sent delegates to the convention except for Rhode Island. Fifty-five men took part. One was George Washington, who became the president of the convention. Others were Alexander Hamilton, James Madison, and Ben Franklin.

PROBLEMS WITH THE ARTICLES

The Articles of Confederation went into effect in 1781. This constitution gave Congress some powers on paper. However, the state governments still didn't pay attention to it. Congress couldn't make states give it money to take care of national business. The states even dealt with other countries on their own.

Working for Approval

When it came time to sign the new U.S. Constitution, however, some delegates wouldn't do it. They still thought the federal government was too strong. Some wanted a bill of rights to **protect** people. They wanted to limit the government's power. The Constitution was then sent to the states to be ratified, or approved. Some states also **demanded** a bill of rights first.

Some delegates promised to add this list. By June 1788, enough states had ratified the Constitution to make it law.

Some people worked hard to get state leaders to ratify the Constitution. Among them were James Madison, Alexander Hamilton, and John Jay (shown). The three men wrote the 85 **essays** of the Federalist papers. These essays explained the new constitution.

STATES AND RATIFICATION

Nine of the 13 states needed to ratify the U.S. Constitution. Here's the timeline:

December 7, 1787 • **Delaware**
December 12, 1787 • **Pennsylvania**
December 18, 1787 • **New Jersey**
January 2, 1788 • **Georgia**
January 9, 1788 • **Connecticut**
February 6, 1788 • **Massachusetts**
April 28, 1788 • **Maryland**
May 23, 1788 • **South Carolina**
June 21, 1788 • **New Hampshire**
June 25, 1788 • **Virginia**
June 26, 1788 • **New York**
November 21, 1789 • **North Carolina**
May 29, 1790 • **Rhode Island**

A List of Rights

James Madison was a convention delegate and then congressman. At first, he didn't think a bill of rights was needed. In time, he changed his mind and created the first list of these rights. He presented the list to Congress in 1789. By the end of 1791, the states had approved the 10 amendments that make up the U.S. Bill of Rights.

These amendments protect rights such as freedom of speech, the press, and religion; the right to bear arms; protections for property; and protections for those accused of crimes.

OTHER AMENDMENTS

The U.S. Constitution has been amended many times since the Bill of Rights was created. The most recent amendment is the 27th Amendment, approved in 1992.

VERIFIED

The National Constitution Center aims to teach people about the U.S. Constitution. Find out more at **constitutioncenter.org**.

James Madison later became the fourth president of the United States in 1809.

An Incomplete List

There are a few reasons why some people once argued against a bill of rights. One is that no list of rights could ever be complete. It was impossible to include everything. And the government could someday say that since a specific right wasn't included, it didn't exist.

The Ninth Amendment (and then the Tenth Amendment) was meant to work against this. It says that the rights named in the rest of the amendments aren't alone. People have other rights too.

A DIFFERENT AMENDMENT

Unlike the first eight amendments, the Ninth Amendment is fairly unspecific. It states a general rule for the people and the government. It warns that the list is not complete.

THE NINTH AMENDMENT

"The enumeration (listing) in the Constitution, of certain rights, shall not be construed (taken) to deny (take away) or disparage (hurt) others retained (kept) by the people."

Alexander Hamilton once said the following about a bill of rights: "Why declare that things shall not be done which there is no power to do?"

Powers Divided

In some ways, the Tenth Amendment is much like the Ninth. It's not as specific as earlier amendments. It doesn't name certain rights. It says that the powers not given to the federal government by the Constitution are kept for the states. (But it doesn't include powers specifically kept from the states by the Constitution.)

The amendment has no specific limits for the federal government. It doesn't give the states more powers. It does let the states create their own laws unless they go against federal laws.

PATRICK HENRY

Patrick Henry (1736–1799) was a Founding Father involved in the **American Revolution**. He was a supporter of states' rights. He didn't support the U.S. Constitution. He thought it would hurt the states and people's rights.

THE TENTH AMENDMENT

"The powers not delegated (given) to the United States by the Constitution, nor prohibited (kept away) by it to the States, are reserved to the States respectively, or to the people."

Vermont was the 14th state to be added to the United States. It was the first after the original 13 colonies. It entered in 1791, the same year the Bill of Rights was ratified.

Similarities

The Ninth and Tenth Amendments are similar in a few ways. They both limit the powers of the federal government. They both came from the **debates** about whether a bill of rights should be added to the Constitution at all. They're meant to show that there are many rights, although they're not all spelled out in the Constitution.

The amendments are sometimes considered safety nets for the rights of people and states. They work together to provide a balance of powers.

JOHN LOCKE

John Locke (1632–1704) was an English **philosopher**. He wrote about the consent of the governed. His thoughts were important to the writers of the Constitution and Bill of Rights. He said that all people are born with certain rights.

CONSENT OF THE GOVERNED

The idea that government gets its power from the consent, or agreement, of the governed is important to the United States. Many people have written about this idea for many years. Without this consent, this idea says, government loses **legitimacy**.

Thomas Hobbes (1588–1679) was another English philosopher. Like Locke, he also wrote about the consent of the governed.

Interpretations

Both the Ninth and Tenth Amendments can be subject to strict or loose **interpretations**. (This is true of the rest of the Constitution and Bill of Rights too.) In this **context**, "strict" means based on the exact words of these documents. Changes through history don't matter in this interpretation.

"Loose" means allowing freedom to interpret the documents. This is based on the needs of the time and the people. This also includes new information, or facts. These interpretations can greatly change the way people think of these amendments.

ORIGINALISM

Originalism is a legal, or law-related, way of thinking. It says that the words of the Constitution should be interpreted as they were at the time they were written. It doesn't matter that they were written in the 1780s.

HAMILTON VS. JEFFERSON AND MADISON

Alexander Hamilton leaned toward a loose interpretation of the Constitution. Thomas Jefferson and James Madison thought it should be interpreted strictly. Hamilton wanted to create a national bank. Jefferson and Madison said the federal government had no power to do so.

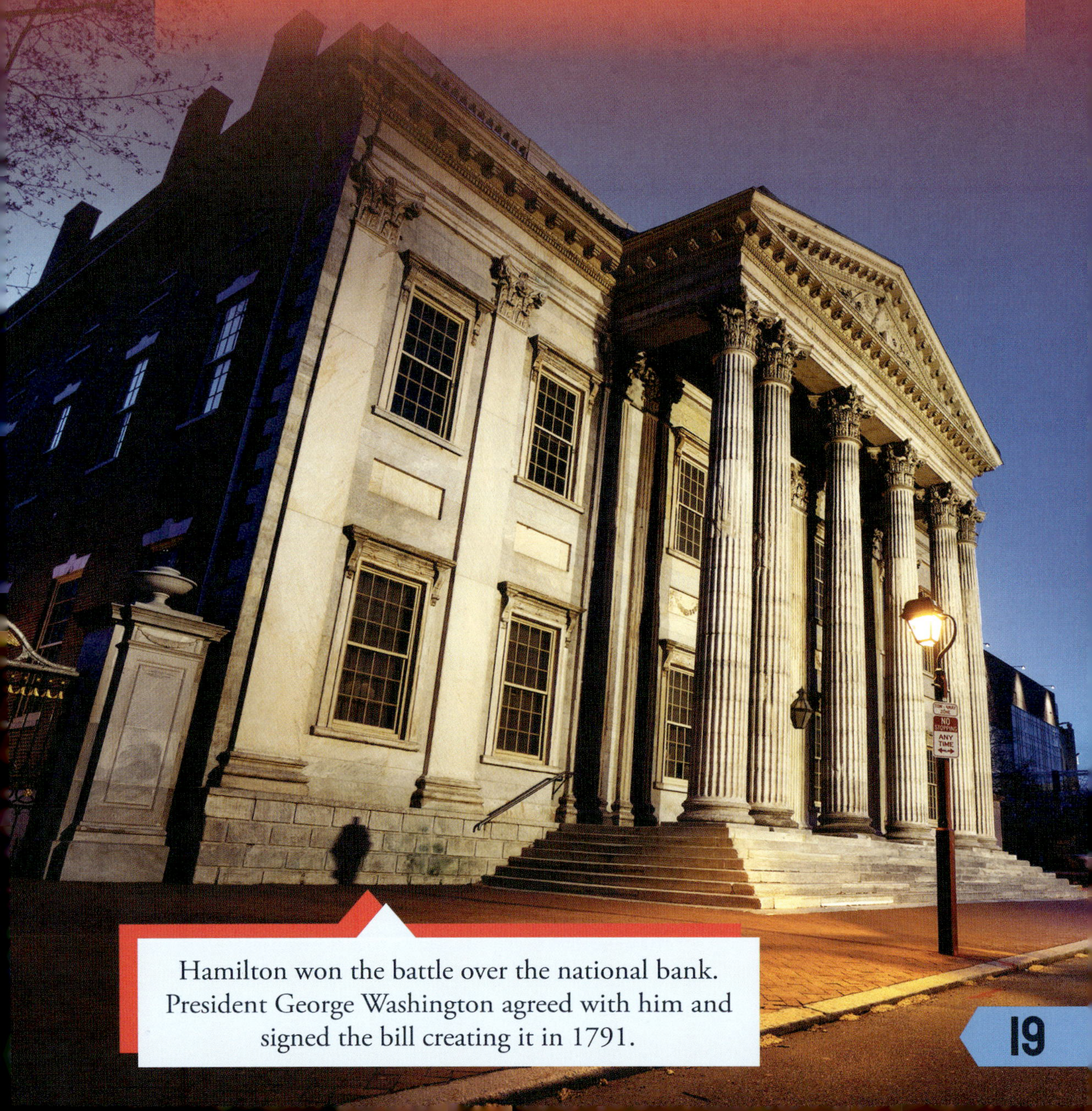

Hamilton won the battle over the national bank. President George Washington agreed with him and signed the bill creating it in 1791.

The Part of the Courts

Because the Ninth and Tenth Amendments aren't very specific, it's been up to the courts of the United States to decide what they mean to U.S. citizens. This means what rights the Ninth Amendment does or doesn't protect. It also means deciding what the federal government can do. It also decides what falls to the states.

Early on, people sometimes tried to use the amendments to **challenge** federal government actions. They'd say these actions weren't constitutional. The Supreme Court generally turned these challenges aside.

HATCH POLITICAL ACTIVITY ACT

In 1947, the Supreme Court dismissed challenges to the Hatch Political Activity Act. The challenges tried to use these amendments. The act is a federal law that bans some federal government workers from taking part in political activity.

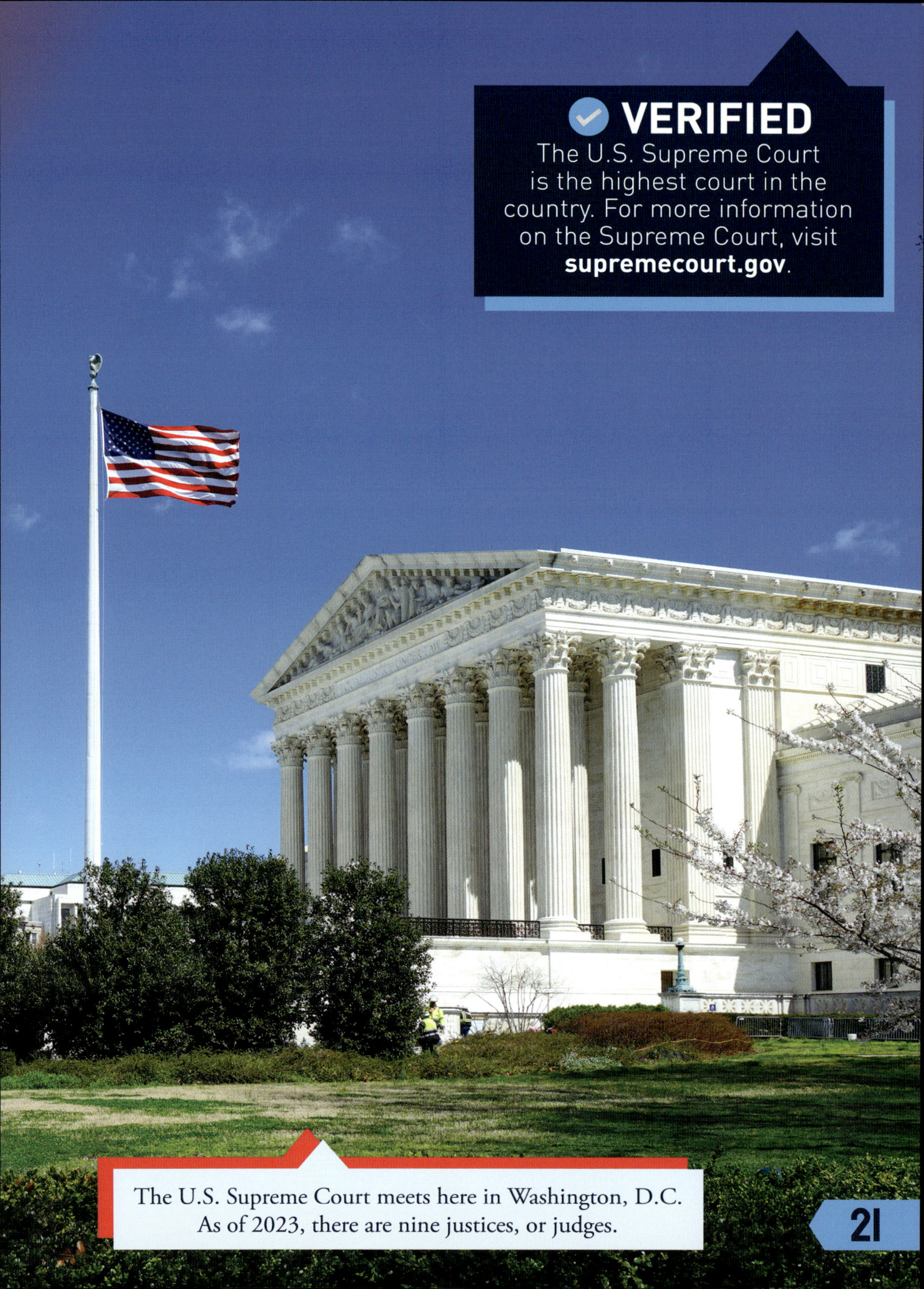

VERIFIED
The U.S. Supreme Court is the highest court in the country. For more information on the Supreme Court, visit **supremecourt.gov**.

The U.S. Supreme Court meets here in Washington, D.C. As of 2023, there are nine justices, or judges.

The Ninth in the Courts

The U.S. Supreme Court didn't cite, or name, the Ninth Amendment much in the early history of the country. That changed in the 20th century. A case called *Griswold v. Connecticut* reached the Supreme Court in 1965. At the time, the state had laws that said people couldn't use **contraception**.

The Supreme Court decided the law was unconstitutional. This was only when applied to married couples, though. It ruled that people had the right to expect privacy when it came to their marriage.

AMENDMENTS AND *GRISWOLD*

The Supreme Court used the Fourth and Fifth Amendments. It said they showed people had a right to privacy. It used the Ninth Amendment as a basis too. Justice Arthur Goldberg wrote about it. He said the amendment shows there are "additional **fundamental** rights" beyond the Bill of Rights.

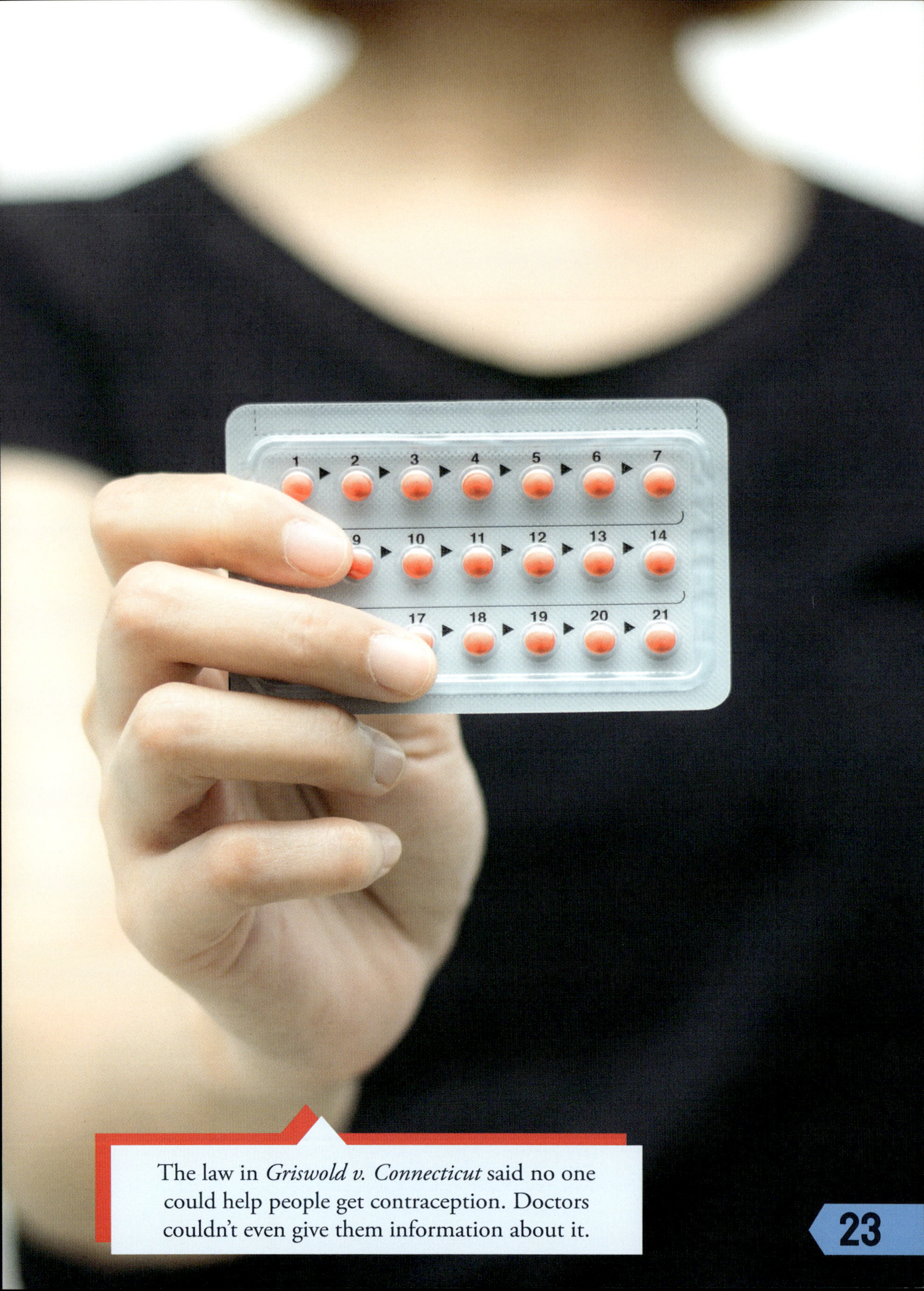

The law in *Griswold v. Connecticut* said no one could help people get contraception. Doctors couldn't even give them information about it.

Roe v. Wade

In 1973, the Supreme Court mentioned the Ninth Amendment again. This was in its decision in the case *Roe v. Wade*. This case dealt with a person's right to have an **abortion**. The court said that state laws that overly limit abortion rights are unconstitutional.

The court said the due process clause, or part, of the Fourteenth Amendment protects personal freedoms and choices. It also mentioned the Ninth Amendment and *Griswold*. It said "a right of personal privacy" exists under the Constitution.

THE *DOBBS* CASE

In 2022, the Supreme Court overturned *Roe v. Wade*. It did this in the case *Dobbs v. Jackson Women's Health Organization*. However, the justices noted that cases such as *Griswold* still stood.

DUE PROCESS

The due process clause of the Fourteenth Amendment is important. It says that no one should be "**deprived** of life, liberty, or property without due process of law." "Due process" means fairness under the law and the protection of rights.

Many people **protested** after the Supreme Court overturned *Roe v. Wade*.

A Guideline

Federal courts have used the Ninth Amendment as a guideline in decisions. However, it's never been the main part of any decision. In another example, the Supreme Court mentioned it in a ruling in 1980. The case was *Richmond Newspapers Inc. v. Virginia*. The court said the public has a right to attend **criminal trials**.

This right is mainly guaranteed, or promised, by the First and Fourteenth Amendments. But the court held that it was backed up by the Ninth Amendment.

FIRST AMENDMENT

The First Amendment to the U.S. Constitution promises the freedom of speech. It also promises other freedoms. These include freedom of the press and freedom of religion.

VERIFIED
The Freedom of the Press Foundation protects and defends, or stands up for, the rights of the First Amendment. To learn more, visit **freedom.press**.

The *Richmond Newspapers Inc. v. Virginia* case started when a judge closed a trial to the public. Reporters at the court said trials shouldn't be closed to them or others.

A Change from the Articles

The Tenth Amendment doesn't put any specific limits on the federal government. It's very much like part of the Articles of Confederation. However, the Articles had the word "**expressly**" in front of the word "delegated" in that sentence. (As well as a few other differences.)

Some people wanted to add this word in the same place in the Tenth Amendment. That would have done away with the idea of **implied** powers for the federal government. Congress refused to add it.

VERIFIED

The Bill of Rights Institute is a nonprofit group. It aims to teach people about the Bill of Rights and civics. "Civics" means the rights and duties of citizens and how government works. Find out more at **billofrightsinstitute.org**.

Elbridge Gerry (1744–1814) was one of those who tried to add "expressly" to the Tenth Amendment. He'd also refused to sign the Constitution. He was later vice president from 1813 to 1814.

Early Cases

Early on, some states tried to test the "necessary and proper" clause of the Constitution. They tested it against the Tenth Amendment. The clause says that Congress has the power to make all laws that are "necessary and proper" to help carry out its duties.

In 1819, the Supreme Court ruled in the case *McCulloch v. Maryland*. It said that Congress has implied powers beyond its listed powers. This was true so it could do its job. It was true even though the Tenth Amendment exists.

JOHN MARSHALL

John Marshall (1755–1835) was a founder of the United States. He was the fourth chief justice of the Supreme Court. He was very important to founding the U.S. law system. He took part in more than 1,000 legal decisions. This includes *McCulloch v. Maryland*.

John Marshall was chief justice from 1801 to 1835. He's considered one of the most important chief justices in U.S. history.

A Civil War

The Supreme Court didn't bring up the Tenth Amendment much again until the early 20th century. However, the idea of states' rights affected the country in a big way in the later 1800s. In 1861, the American Civil War started. Eleven Southern states left the Union and started the Confederate States of America.

These states fought for the right to protect slavery. They thought they should be able to own people. They were afraid the federal government would end this.

"NOT EQUAL"

Alexander Stephens was the vice president of the Confederate States. He said that the Confederacy was based on "the great truth, that the [Black man] is not equal to the white man; that slavery ... is his natural and normal condition."

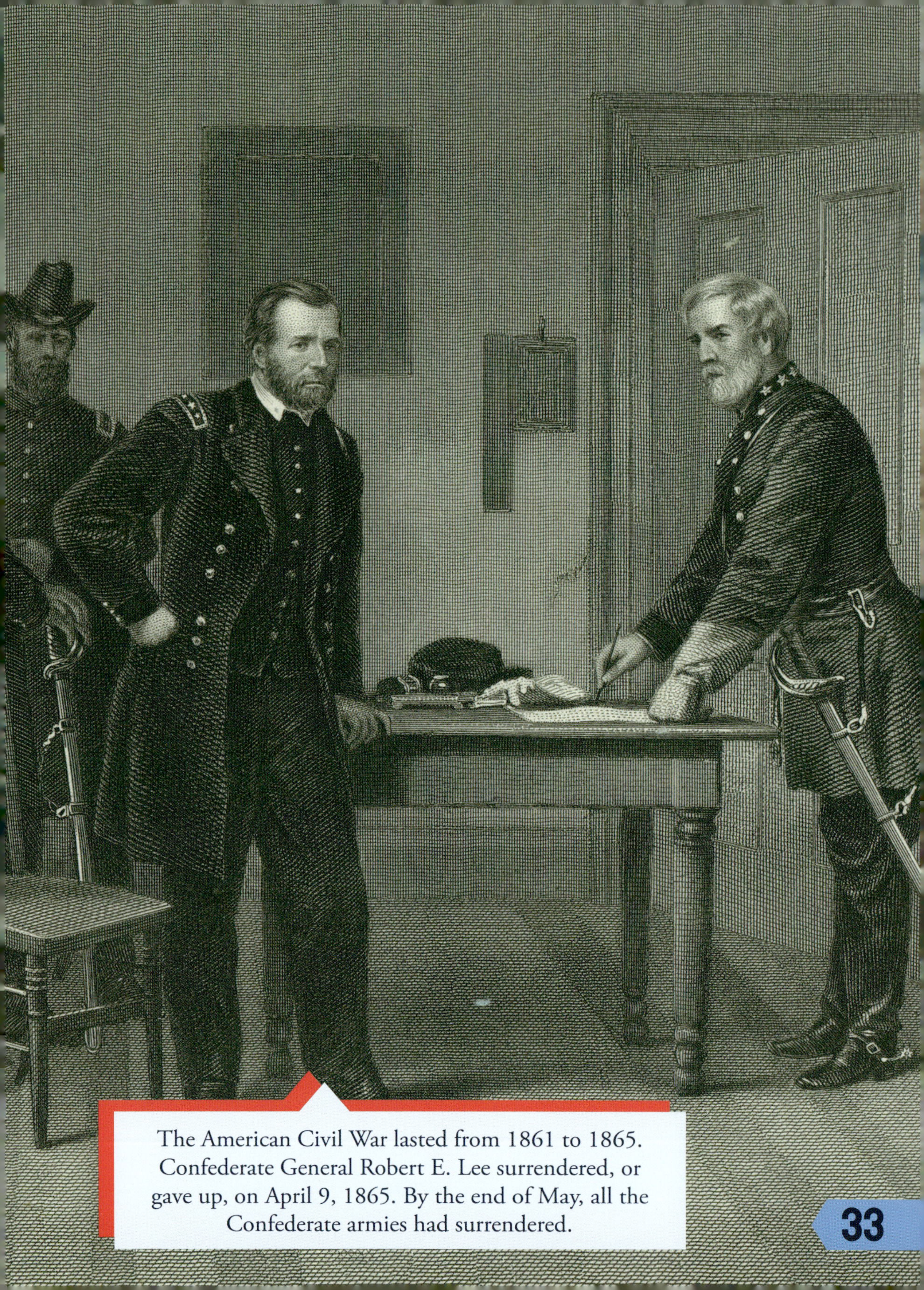

The American Civil War lasted from 1861 to 1865. Confederate General Robert E. Lee surrendered, or gave up, on April 9, 1865. By the end of May, all the Confederate armies had surrendered.

The 20th Century

At the start of the 20th century, the Supreme Court used the Tenth Amendment to rule against some federal laws. These laws were often about **economic** activity. One federal law was meant to limit child labor. It would stop companies from shipping goods made by child workers.

In 1918, the Supreme Court said that this law wasn't constitutional. It said it went beyond the powers of the federal government. It said the states should decide about child labor.

THE PROGRESSIVE ERA

Efforts to end child labor came from ideas during the Progressive Era of the United States. This was a time of spreading social **activism**. People worked against poverty, or the state of being poor. They also worked to end corruption. This means dishonest or illegal behavior by powerful people.

The child labor case in 1918 is called *Hammer v. Dagenhart*. The court would go on to use the Tenth Amendment to rule against other federal laws. It said they went against state powers.

The Darby Case

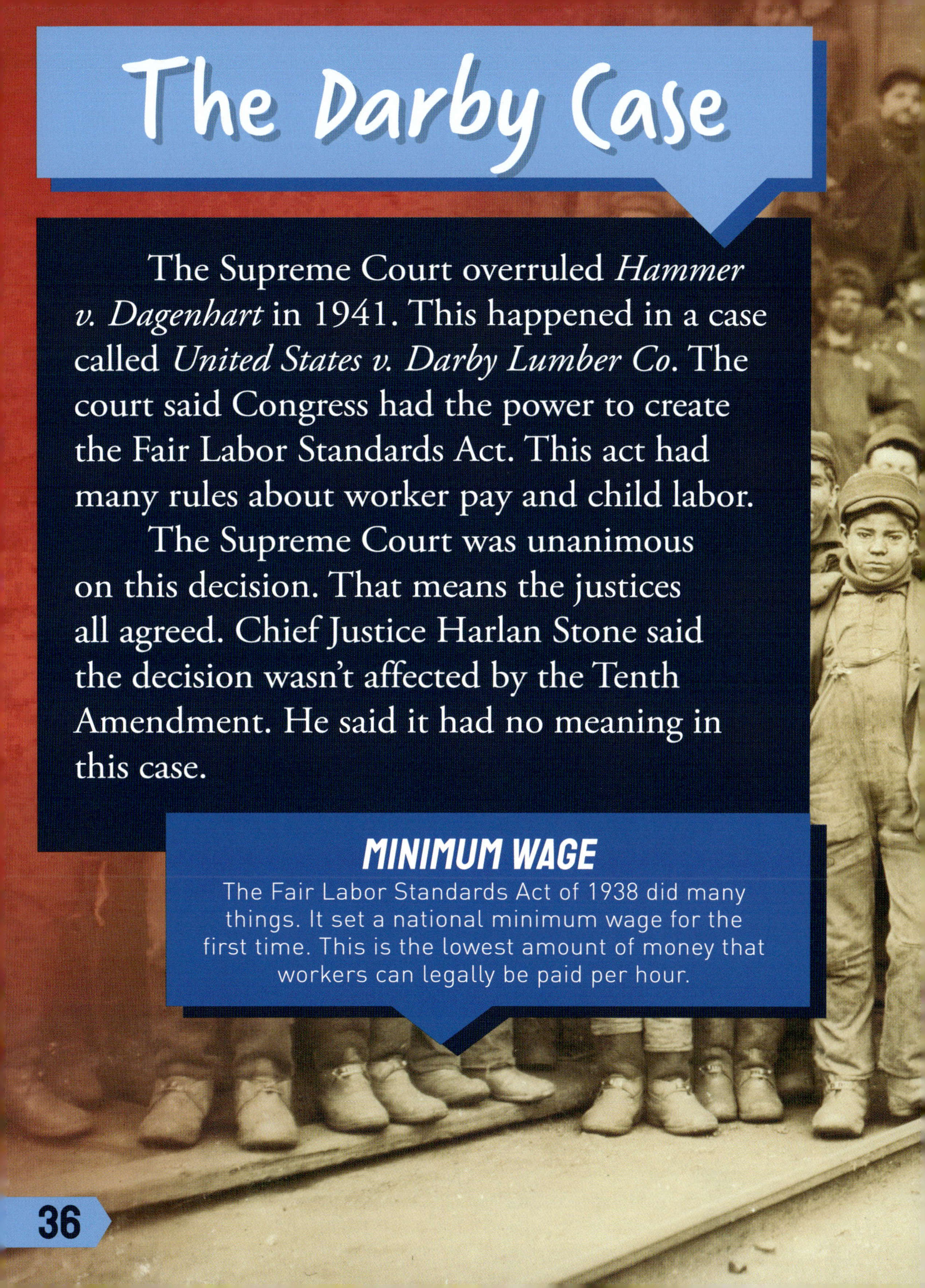

The Supreme Court overruled *Hammer v. Dagenhart* in 1941. This happened in a case called *United States v. Darby Lumber Co.* The court said Congress had the power to create the Fair Labor Standards Act. This act had many rules about worker pay and child labor.

The Supreme Court was unanimous on this decision. That means the justices all agreed. Chief Justice Harlan Stone said the decision wasn't affected by the Tenth Amendment. He said it had no meaning in this case.

MINIMUM WAGE

The Fair Labor Standards Act of 1938 did many things. It set a national minimum wage for the first time. This is the lowest amount of money that workers can legally be paid per hour.

VERIFIED

Child labor is still a big problem around the world. About 160 million children from ages 5 to 17 are part of it. One group working to stop this is the Global March Against Child Labour. Find out more at **globalmarch.org**.

The Fair Labor Standards Act helped child workers in the United States. It said that children under 16 couldn't work in mining or manufacturing fields. These were the most dangerous, or unsafe, jobs.

After Darby

In the years after *Darby*, the Supreme Court kept much the same interpretation. It dismissed other cases that tried to use the Tenth Amendment to go against federal laws.

Starting in the mid-1970s, things changed somewhat. The court began using the amendment to look at some federal laws. It decided if these laws went against state sovereignty. This is the power and duty of a state to govern itself. That's without the federal government getting in the way too much.

THE *GARCIA* CASE

Garcia v. San Antonio Metropolitan Transit Authority was a Supreme Court case in 1986. The court found state sovereignty was protected enough by the Constitution itself. The Tenth Amendment doesn't have to come into it.

TAXATION

During this time, many cases often had to do with economic matters again. Some had to do with taxation. This is the action of taxing people or things. That means making people pay money that then goes toward things done by the government.

The *Garcia* case was about pay for workers in San Antonio, Texas. "Metropolitan" means having to do with a large city. "Transit" means having to do with moving people or things.

In the 1990s

Starting in the 1990s, the Supreme Court started using the Tenth Amendment more. The cases often had to do with times the federal government told states to do something. This could mean passing certain laws.

In 1992, the court ruled on the case *New York v. United States*. It said the federal government can't force states to "enact or **enforce**" a federal program. To "enact" means to make it part of their law.

THE *PRINTZ* CASE

The *Printz v. United States* case was decided in 1997. The Supreme Court said the Brady Law went against the Tenth Amendment. This law said local police had to do checks on gun buyers.

COMMANDEERING

The doctrine, or rule, in this case is called the anti-commandeering doctrine. To commandeer something means to take it over.

The *New York v. United States* case had to do with **radioactive** waste. The government wanted states to do something about this waste.

The Commerce Clause

"Commerce" means activities having to do with business. The commerce clause of the Constitution gives Congress the power to make rules about this. Several times in the past 30 years, the Supreme Court has said the Tenth Amendment limits this power.

In 1995, the court struck down a federal law in *United States v. Lopez*. This law set gun-free zones, or areas, in and around schools. The government said it could do this because of the economic effects of guns. The court disagreed.

THE *MORRISON* CASE

In 2000, the Supreme Court again struck down part of a federal law with the Tenth Amendment. The case was *United States v. Morrison*. The court said part of the **Violence** Against Women Act went past Congress's power.

VERIFIED

The Brady Law was named for James Brady, a politician who was shot in 1981. The Brady organization works against gun violence in the United States. For more information, visit **bradyunited.org**.

After the *Lopez* case, laws changed so some gun-free zones in schools were allowed. You may have seen signs like this in your school.

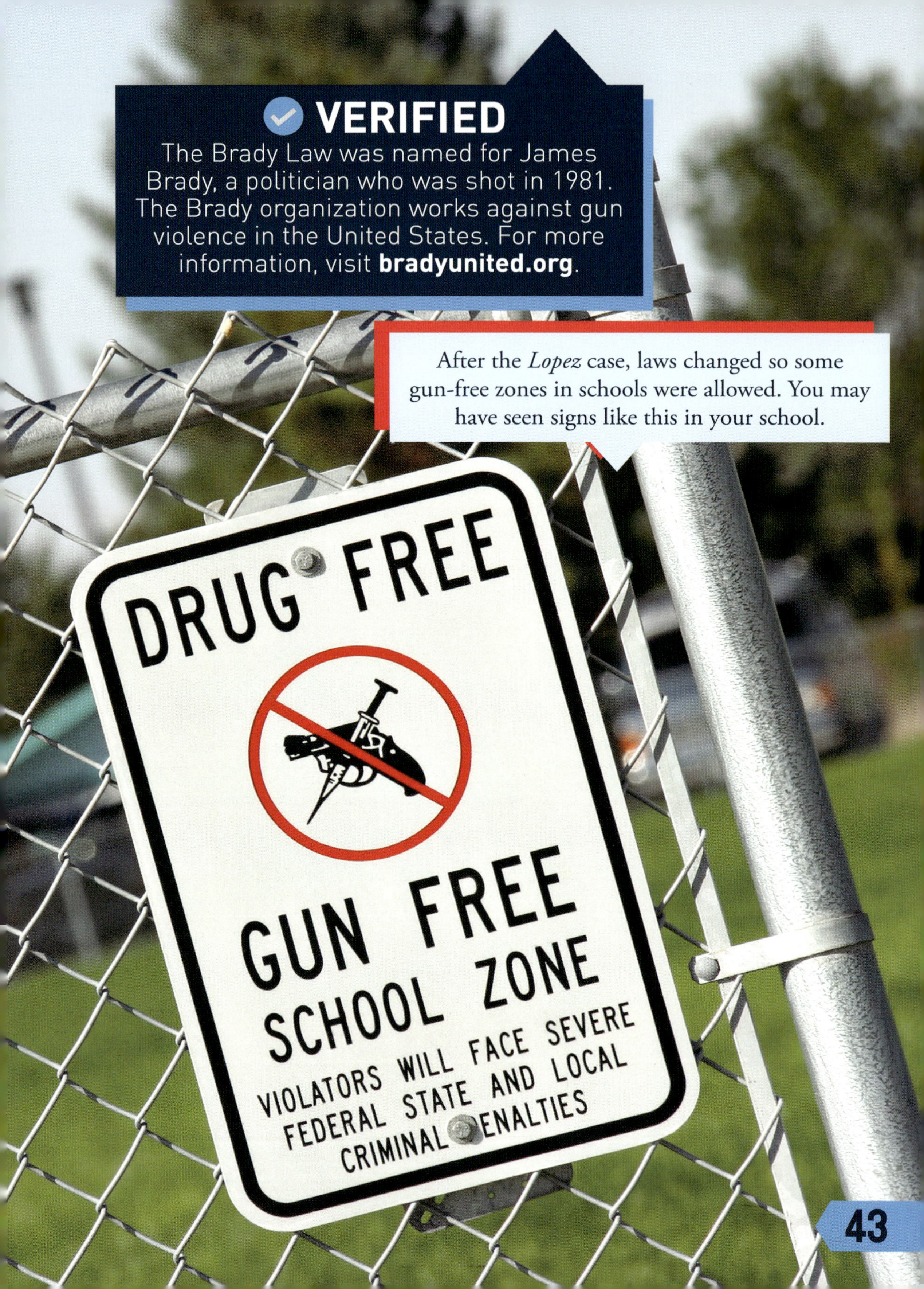

The Future

More than 200 years after they were written, the Ninth and Tenth Amendments still affect the government today. So do the ideas of the rights of the people and the states. The balance between these rights and powers of government will continue to be important.

In 2020, the COVID-19 **pandemic** threw more challenges at this balance. Many people were very confused. What safety measures could governments—state or federal—put in place? Could one government do away with these measures? Could they be enforced? Some people or states didn't want to follow them. Others wanted stricter measures. Years after the start of the pandemic, there's still confusion.

Different states dealt with COVID-19 in very different ways. For example, states with a lot of people had different needs than states with fewer people.

As we move further into the 21st century, there are sure to be more challenges. States have been taking on more power and challenging more federal laws. People still have far different ideas about how these amendments are supposed to work. What do you think will happen next?

GLOSSARY

abortion: The act of stopping a pregnancy.

activism: Acting strongly in support of or against an issue.

American Revolution: A war that lasted from 1775 to 1783 in which the American colonists won independence from British rule.

challenge: To question the power or actions of someone, or the action of doing so.

constitution: The basic laws by which a country, state, or group is governed.

context: The situation in which something happens.

contraception: Methods of birth control to prevent pregnancy.

convention: A gathering of people who have a common interest or purpose.

criminal trial: A meeting in a court in which information is presented to judge or jury so decisions can be made about the law having to do with a crime.

debate: A talk between people who have different opinions about something.

delegate: A person sent to a meeting or convention to represent others.

demand: A strong request for something, or make a strong request for something.

deprive: To take something away from someone, to keep it from someone.

economic: Having to do with the economy, or the system or process by which goods and services are made, sold, and bought in an area.

enforce: To make sure people follow a rule or law.

essay: A short piece of writing about a person's thoughts.

expressly: In a very clear, definite way.

fundamental: Relating to or forming the most important, basic part of things.

imply: To say or suggest something in an indirect way.

interpretation: The act of explaining something, often in different ways.

legitimacy: The state of being legitimate, or real, accepted, or official.

pandemic: An occurrence in which a disease spreads quickly to multiple countries around the world at the same time and affects many people at once.

philosopher: Someone who seeks wisdom or enlightenment.

protect: To keep safe.

protest: An event at which a group objects to an idea, an act, or a way of doing something; to strongly oppose something.

radioactive: Giving off rays of light, heat, or energy.

rebellion: A fight to overthrow a government.

specific: Clearly and exactly presented or stated.

violence: The use of bodily force to hurt, harm, or destroy.

INDEX